VETERINARIANS

BY EMMA LESS

AMICUS READERS ● AMICUS INK

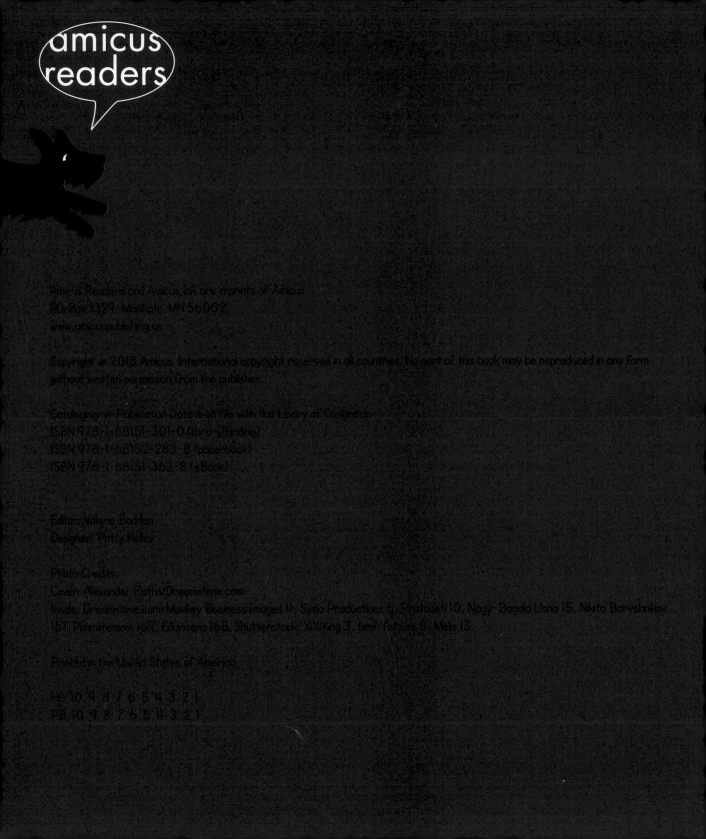

amicus
readers

Amicus Readers and Amicus Ink are imprints of Amicus
PO Box 1329 Mankato, MN 56002
www.amicuspublishing.us

Cataloging-in-Publication Data is on file with the Library of Congress.
ISBN 978-1-68151-301-0 (library binding)
ISBN 978-1-68152-283-8 (paperback)
ISBN 978-1-68151-363-8 (eBook)

Editor: Valerie Bodden
Designer: Patty Kelley

Photo Credits:
Cover: Alexander Raths/Dreamstime.com
Inside: Dreamstime.com: Monkey Business Images 4, Syda Productions 6, Photodeti 10, Nagy-Bagoly Ilona 15, Nikita Baryshnikov 16T, Pimmimemom 16R, Eduniwero 16B, Shutterstock: XiXiXing 3, bmf-foto.de 8, Mitis 13

Printed in the United States of America.

HC 10 9 8 7 6 5 4 3 2 1
PB 10 9 8 7 6 5 4 3 2 1

Vets take care of animals.

The vet checks
Tim's dog.
He looks at its ears.

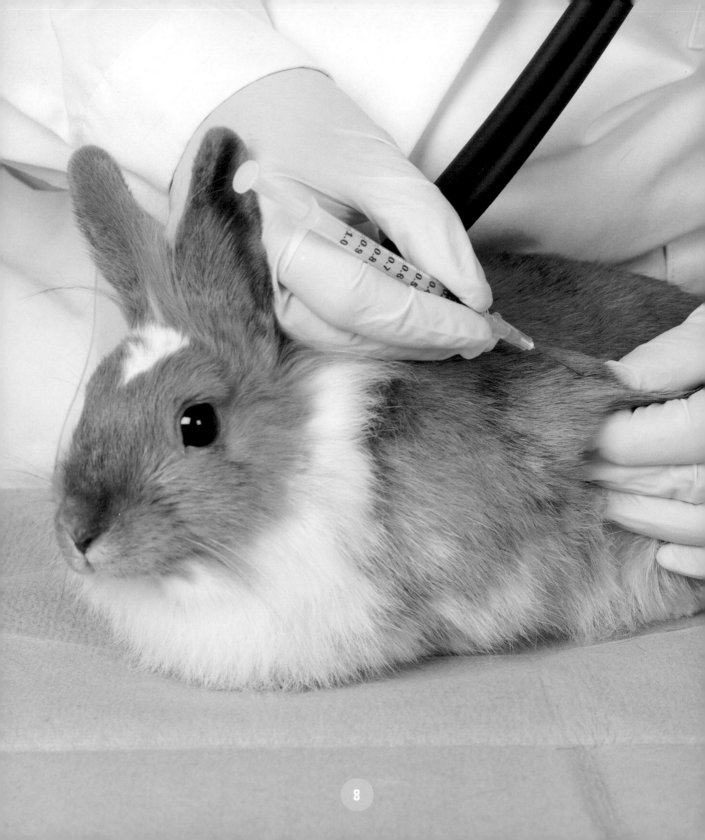

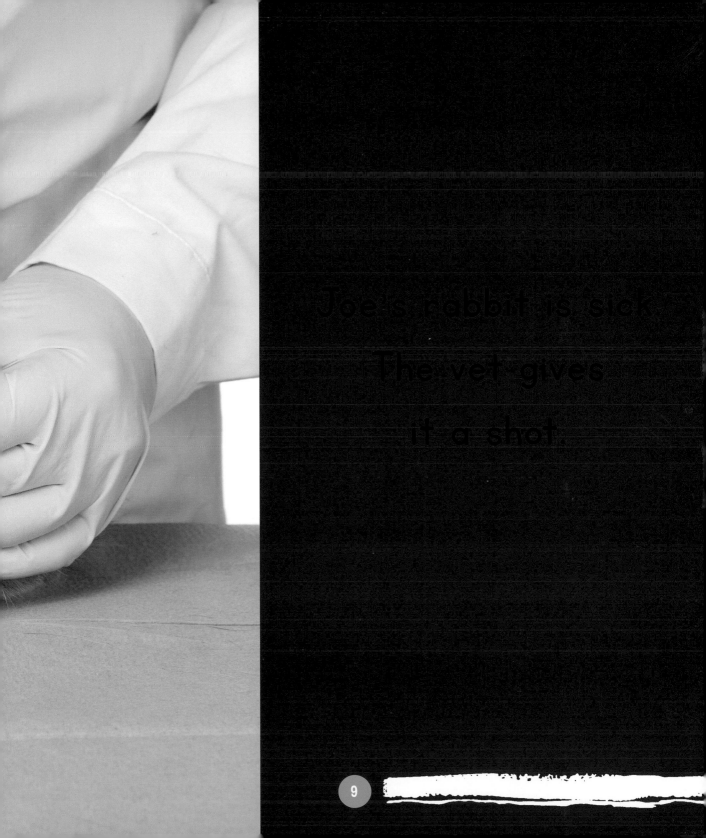

Joe's rabbit is sick.
The vet gives
it a shot.

Donna brings
in her cat.
It will have kittens!

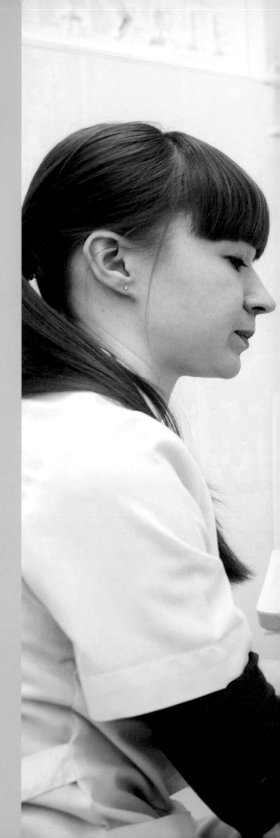

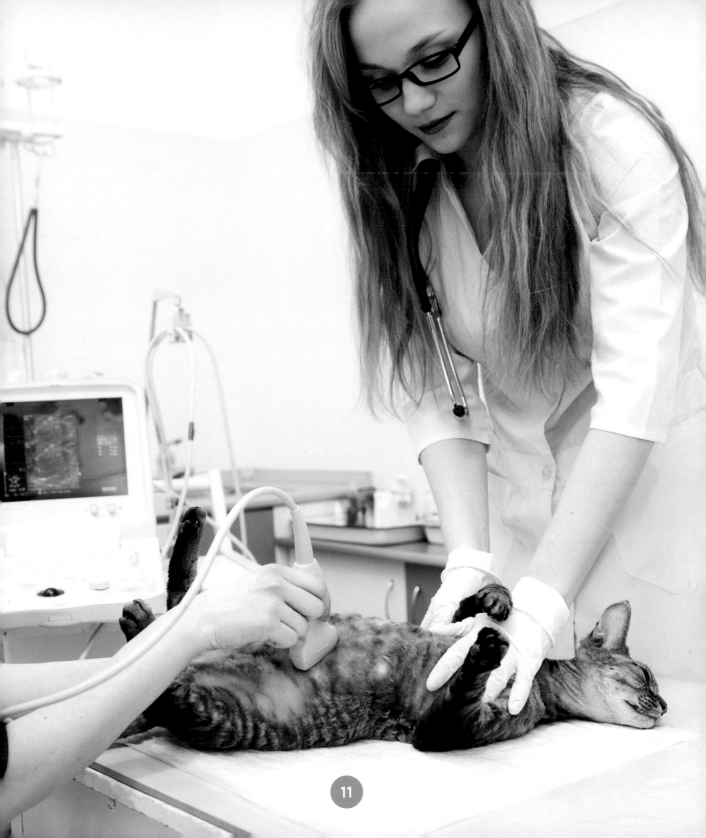

This vet looks at Jim's horse. He checks the horse's feet.

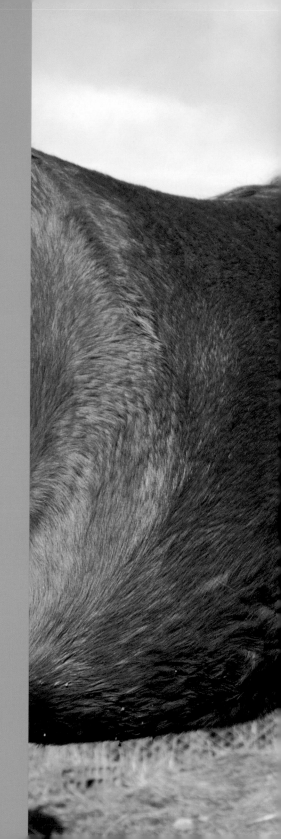

Vets keep
our pets healthy!

SEEN AT THE VET'S OFFICE

pet toys

pet food

medicine

FOR ANIMAL USE ONLY

HOLD TAB DOWN & TURN